First World War
and Army of Occupation
War Diary
France, Belgium and Germany

4 CAVALRY DIVISION
Divisional Troops
4 Field Squadron Royal Engineers
1 January 1917 - 20 April 1918

WO95/1158/4

The Naval & Military Press Ltd
www.nmarchive.com
Published in association with The National Archives

Published by

The Naval & Military Press Ltd

Unit 10 Ridgewood Industrial Park,

Uckfield, East Sussex,

TN22 5QE England

Tel: +44 (0) 1825 749494

www.naval-military-press.com

www.nmarchive.com

This diary has been reprinted in facsimile from the original. Any imperfections are inevitably reproduced and the quality may fall short of modern type and cartographic standards.

© **Crown Copyright**
Images reproduced by permission of The National Archives, London, England, 2015.

Contents

Document type	Place/Title	Date From	Date To
Heading	WO95/1158/4		
Heading	1917-18 4th Cavalry Division 4th Field Sqdn R.E. Jan 1917-Apl 1918		
Miscellaneous	47d Sqdn RE		
Heading	War Diary of 4th Field Squadron, R.E. From 1st January 1917 To 31st January 1917		
War Diary	Boismont	01/01/1917	31/01/1917
Heading	4th Field Squadron R.E. 1st to 28th February 1917		
War Diary	Boismont	01/02/1917	28/02/1917
Heading	4th Field Squadron R.E. from 1st to 31st March 1917		
Miscellaneous	Issued to Section		
War Diary	Boismont	01/03/1917	18/03/1917
War Diary	Buigny-St-Mallou	19/03/1917	19/03/1917
War Diary	Bonneville	20/03/1917	20/03/1917
War Diary	Albert	21/03/1917	22/03/1917
War Diary	Irles	23/03/1917	05/04/1917
War Diary	Bihucourt	06/04/1917	10/04/1917
Heading	4th Field Squadron, R.E. from 1st to 30th April 1917		
Miscellaneous	Issued to Section		
War Diary	Bihucourt	11/04/1917	13/04/1917
War Diary	Marieux	14/04/1917	30/04/1917
Heading	War Diary 4th Field Squadron. B.E. 4th Cavalry Division W.D 4/17 April 1917		
Heading	4th Field Squadron, R.E. from 1st may to 30th June 1917		
Miscellaneous	Issued to Section		
War Diary	Marieux	01/05/1917	08/05/1917
War Diary	Meaulte	09/05/1917	09/05/1917
War Diary	Brie	10/05/1917	11/05/1917
War Diary	Fourques	12/05/1917	23/05/1917
War Diary	Roisel	24/05/1917	30/06/1917
Heading	4th Field Squadron, R.E. from 1st to 31st July 1917		
Miscellaneous	Issued to Section		
War Diary	Roisel	01/07/1917	08/07/1917
War Diary	Fourques	09/07/1917	31/07/1917
Heading	4th Field Squadron, R.E. from 1st to 31st August 1917		
War Diary	Fourques	01/08/1917	21/11/1917
War Diary	Fins	22/11/1917	23/11/1917
War Diary	Fourques	24/11/1917	29/11/1917
War Diary	Villers Foucon	30/11/1917	03/12/1917
War Diary	Heudicourt	04/12/1917	06/12/1917
War Diary	Fourques	07/12/1917	13/02/1918
War Diary	Devise	14/02/1918	22/02/1918
War Diary	Brusle	23/02/1918	13/03/1918
War Diary	Brie	14/03/1918	14/03/1918
War Diary	Blangy-Tronville	15/03/1918	15/03/1918
War Diary	Ferribres	16/03/1918	16/03/1918
War Diary	Bettencourt	17/03/1918	26/03/1918
War Diary	Famechon	27/03/1918	27/03/1918
War Diary	Ailly Le Haut Clocher	28/03/1918	20/04/1918

WO 95/158/4

1917-18
4TH CAVALRY DIVISION

4TH FIELD SQDN R.E.
JAN 1917-APL 1918.

467th Squadr RE

SERIAL NO. 14 8

Confidential

War Diary

of

4TH FIELD SQUADRON, R.E.

FROM 1st JANUARY 1917 191

TO 31st JANUARY 1917 191

Confidential

Army Form C. 2118

WAR DIARY
or
INTELLIGENCE SUMMARY

(Erase heading not required.)

Instructions regarding War Diaries and Intelligence Summaries are contained in F.S. Regs., Part II. and the Staff Manual respectively. Title Pages will be prepared in manuscript.

Place	Date	Hour	Summary of Events and Information	Remarks and references to Appendices
BOISMONT	1.1.17		Squadron employed on billetting work	Q1NK
"	2.1.17		ditto	Q1NK
	3.1.17		ditto	Q1NK
	4.1.17		ditto	Q1NK
	5.1.17		ditto	Q1NK
	6.1.17		Squadron inspected by Maj. Gen. A. Kennedy C.M.G. 4th Cavalry Division — B Troop completed in machine guns remainder in drill order.	M0K
	7.1.17		Squadron employed on billetting work.	Q1OK
	8.1.17		ditto. B Troop commenced training	
			Drivers Drill, musketry, & physical training for Drivers commenced.	Q1NK
	9.1.17		ditto	Q1NK
	10.1.17		ditto	Q1NK
	11.1.17		ditto	Q1NK
	12.1.17		ditto	Q1NK
	13.1.17		ditto	Q1NK
	14.1.17		ditto	Q1NK
	15.1.17		ditto	Q1NK
	16.1.17		ditto	N1NK

Army Form C. 2118

WAR DIARY or INTELLIGENCE SUMMARY

(Erase heading not required.)

Place	Date	Hour	Summary of Events and Information	Remarks and references to Appendices
BOISMONT	17.1.17.		Billeting work. B Troop, 1st Drivers continue training	nil.
	18.1.17		ditto	nil.
	19.1.17		ditto	nil.
	20.1.17		ditto	nil.
	21.1.17		Major R.M.T. KERR proceeds to LE PARCQ for course of instruction at R.E. School	
	22.1.17		Billeting work. B Troop and Drivers continued training.	
	23.1.17		" "	
	24.1.17		" "	
	25.1.17		" "	
	26.1.17		" "	
	27.1.17		" "	
	28.1.17		" "	
	29.1.17		" "	
	30.1.17		" "	
	31.1.17		27' omis.	

Major Rintoul
O.C. Matthews Major RE
O.C. 4th Field Squadron

Serial No. 148.

4th Field Squadron, R.E.

1st to 28th February 1917.

Army Form C. 2118

WAR DIARY or INTELLIGENCE SUMMARY
(Erase heading not required.)

Instructions regarding War Diaries and Intelligence Summaries are contained in F. S. Regs., Part II. and the Staff Manual respectively. Title Pages will be prepared in manuscript.

4TH FIELD SQUADRON, R.E., 4TH CAVALRY DIVISION.
W.D. 2.
Date FEB. 1917.

Place	Date	Hour	Summary of Events and Information	Remarks and references to Appendices
BOISMONT	1.2.17		B Troop continued Training – Remainder on billetting work. Major Rait Kerr rejoined from R.E. School of Instruction	MOK
	2.2.17		ditto	MOK
	3.2.17		Musketry for trip	MOK
	4.2.17		Lt Gardner took on Instructorship at Divl School from Lt Briggs, appointed to command Cavalry Corps Bridging Park	MOK
	5.2.17		Training & billetting	MOK
	6.2.17		A Troop commenced Musketry	MOK
	7.2.17		A Troop continued Musketry. Bridging train handed over on formation of Cavalry Corps Bridging Park.	MOK
	8.2.17		Training	MOK
	9.2.17		A Troop completed Musketry	MOK
	10.2.17		Training Hqrs & C Troop	MOK
	11.2.17		Training	MOK
	12.2.17		ditto	MOK
	13.2.17		Training	MOK
	14.2.17		Lt Gammon left to attend Bridging course at AIRE. Training	MOK
	15.2.17		Musketry C Troop. Training	MOK

WAR DIARY
or
INTELLIGENCE SUMMARY

(Erase heading not required.)

Army Form C. 2118

Instructions regarding War Diaries and Intelligence Summaries are contained in F.S. Regs., Part II. and the Staff Manual respectively. Title Pages will be prepared in manuscript.

4TH FIELD SQUADRON, R.E.
4TH CAVALRY DIVISION.

Place	Date	Hour	Summary of Events and Information	Remarks and references to Appendices
BOISMONT	16.2.17		Training	M.NK
	17.2.17		Training	M.NK
	18.2.17		Training. New Scheme commenced.	M.NK
	19.2.17		Training	M.NK
	20.2.17		Training	M.NK
	21.2.17		Training	M.NK
	22.2.17		Training	M.NK
	23.2.17		Training	M.NK
	24.2.17		Training Works.	M.NK
	25.2.17		Training	M.NK
	26.2.17		B Trp proceeded on detachment with Enchew Bde & 1st ANZAC CORPS Men. Training	M.NK
	27.2.17		Training	M.NK
	28.2.17		Training — Bridging with Steel Boat Equipment	M.NK

M. MacPherson
Major R.E.
O.C. 4 Fld. Squadron R.E.

Serial No: 148.

4th Field Squadron, R.E.

From 1st to 31st March, 1917.

Daily list o[f]

in Adjutan[t]

Issued to Section_____

From whom.	No. and date of letter received.

WAR DIARY
or
INTELLIGENCE SUMMARY

(Erase heading not required.)

Army Form C. 2118

Instructions regarding War Diaries and Intelligence Summaries are contained in F.S. Regs., Part II. and the Staff Manual respectively. Title Pages will be prepared in manuscript.

Place	Date	Hour	Summary of Events and Information	Remarks and references to Appendices
BOISMONT	1.3.17		Training	MNR
"	2.3.17		"	MNR
"	3.3.17		"	MNR
"	4.3.17		"	MNR
"	5.3.17		"	MNR
"	6.3.17		"	MNR
"	7.3.17		"	MNR
"	8.3.17		"	MNR
"	9.3.17		"	MNR
"	10.3.17		"	MNR
"	11.3.17		"	MNR
"	12.3.17		"	MNR
"	13.3.17		"	MNR
"	14.3.17		"	MNR
"	15.3.17		"	MNR
"	16.3.17		"	MNR
"	17.3.17		"	MNR
"	18.3.17		"	MNR
BUIGNY-ST-MACLOU	19.3.17		Squadron (less B Tp also with Lothian Bde) marched to BUIGNY ST MACLOU. distance 11 miles where it billetted.	MNR
BONNEVILLE	20.3.17		Squadron marched to BONNEVILLE - distance 25 miles - Billetted.	MNR
ALBERT	21.3.17		Squadron marches to camp at L.24.C. distance 25 miles. Heavy rain, then water covered. 13 Echelon held up by heavy roads.	MNR

1875 Wt W593/826 1,000,000 4/15 J.B.C. & A. A.D.S.S./Forms/C. 2118.

WAR DIARY
or
INTELLIGENCE SUMMARY

(Erase heading not required.)

Army Form C. 2118

Instructions regarding War Diaries and Intelligence Summaries are contained in F.S. Regs., Part II. and the Staff Manual respectively. Title Pages will be prepared in manuscript.

Place	Date	Hour	Summary of Events and Information	Remarks and references to Appendices
ALBERT	22.3.17		Squadron rests – Major Park kerr accompanies G.O.C. to look for Brigade Camp in neighbourhood of IRLES.	MNK
IRLES	23.3.17		Squadron marches to camp at IRLES (L 36 c 9.8). Under canvas.	MNK
"	24.3.17		Commenced work on camp approaches and water supply for STALKOT Bde camp.	MNK
"	26.3.17		Carried on work with working parties from Sialkot Bde. Coy Commander visited camp.	MNK
"	26.3.17		Carried on work with working parties from Sialkot Bde. Coy Commander visited camp.	MNK
"	27.3.17		Major Park Kerr visits 1st Army Hqrs & made arrangements for work on water points at SAPIGNIES	MNK
"	28.3.17		Steam for water point. Squadron carries on with camp work.	MNK
"	29.3.17		Lt GARDNER & dismantling party from B.C. troop proceed to camp S & SAPIGNIES & commence work on water point. Squadron works on IRLES–GREVILLERS road.	MNK
"	30.3.17		Both proceeded – working parties being provided by Brig.Mjr. D.M. arrives from trench area.	MNK
"	31.3.17		Lt. proceeds – Lt BENNETT commences Dirt Hd Camp at BIHUCOURT with D.M. & R. Hrs from D.M. & Lucknow Bde.	MNK

1875 Wt W593/826 1,000,000 4/15 J.B.C. & A. A.D.S.S./Forms/C. 2118.

Army Form C. 2118

WAR DIARY
or
INTELLIGENCE SUMMARY
(Erase heading not required.)

4TH
FIELD SQUADRON, R.E.,
4TH CAVALRY DIVISION.

No. ....
Date ....

Instructions regarding War Diaries and Intelligence Summaries are contained in F.S. Regs., Part II. and the Staff Manual respectively. Title Pages will be prepared in manuscript.

Place	Date	Hour	Summary of Events and Information	Remarks and references to Appendices
IRLES	1.4.17		Work on take point SAPIGNIES, DIV H.Q Camp BIHUCOURT, and Return between BIHUCOURT and IRLES	R/OK
IRLES	2.4.17		ditto	O/OK
"	3.4.17		ditto	O/OK
"	4.4.17		ditto	O/OK
"	5.4.17		ditto	O/OK
BIHUCOURT	6.4.17		Squadron went to Camp S.E. of BIHUCOURT — Lt Graham reports on completion of track.	P/OK
"	7.4.17		Lt Bennett & 8 Tmp commenced work on advanced Dvl report cable station E. of MORY on L'HOMME MORT. Ask on front Cavalry track from SAPIGNIES to ECOUST commenced by Lt Bennett, who reports to Lt Hoft from R.E. & B.M's Rly Brdgsm — 6 x A. O.P. S.L. Hoyt to arrange. Track completed by Army to for on top & water S.E of MORY.	A/OK
"	8.4.17		Sgt Lidsons & 4 O.R. Grounds sent to MORY to take no part. Acting D.R.C. Cavalry track continued to Pr to ECOUST D.R.C. track C. And D.R.C. when 2 w/eleven shells	A/OK
"	9.4.17		Work on Cavalry track at 2 a.m on am. of Sukhaleypre & fronwal Rains to for events.	O/OK
"	10.4.17		Squadron reached at 2 am. in am of Sukhaleypre & fronwal positions to Reconn. S.E of MORY where Brigade was instructed Ltgau Lick Ce Radnor with Lt bg Intr Thursday from Milan recent of Squadron reached Camp at 7am Attached to [illegible] PANZER [illegible]	O/OK

Serial No. 148

4th Field Squadron, R.E.

From 1st to 30th April 1917.

Daily list
in Adjuta

Issued to Section

From whom.	No. and date of letter received.

WAR DIARY
or
INTELLIGENCE SUMMARY
(Erase heading not required.)

Army Form C. 2118

4TH FIELD SQUADRON, R.E.,
4TH CAVALRY DIVISION.

Place	Date	Hour	Summary of Events and Information	Remarks and references to Appendices
BIHUCOURT	11.4.17		Squadron again marched to forward position & returned 2.45 a.m. to its old bivouac. B.R. of 19th Corps on the run attacked & STOKES 1 Gun & the Lieut. and from the 1st Cavalry attempt together & 15 Squadron again returned to camp to refill ammunition with supplies from old dump, 2 men & two horses left 20 minutes late for park on 24 hrs & were wounded with enemy strong	
"	12.4.17		Squadron stood fast at Achiet-le-Petit	M.O.K.
"	13.4.17		Recce on inspection — mines returned to horse L. hard ones not so	M.O.K.
MARIEUX	14.4.17		Squadron less 'A' Trp marched to camp at MARIEUX. Lt Graham & A Trp remained at BIHUCOURT with Cavalry regiment of the Sialkot Bde.	M.O.K.
"	15.4.17		Check, equipment etc. & regn'tn settles down to routine. All efforts on conditioning the horses which had suffered severely from the previous 4 weeks incessantly working — the draught horse particularly having suffered from over-expsre., over-work, & lack of exer.	M.O.K.
"	16.4.17		ditto	M.O.K.

WAR DIARY
or
INTELLIGENCE SUMMARY

(Erase heading not required.)

Army Form C. 2118

Place	Date	Hour	Summary of Events and Information	Remarks and references to Appendices
MARIEUX	17.4.17		Conditioning horses. 15 Dismounted men rejoined for works etc	N/Nil
"	18.4.17		ditto & small work undertaken — holes punched at TARSON & electric lighting in MARIEUX CHATEAU.	N/Nil
"	19.4.17		"A" Troop rejoined — their horses in poor condition thro' the trip.	N/Nil
"	20.4.17		Routine.	N/Nil
"	21.4.17		ditto	N/Nil
"	22.4.17		ditto. Remainder of Dismounts men rejoined for works.	N/Nil
"	23.4.17		ditto	N/Nil
"	24.4.17		ditto	N/Nil
"	25.4.17		ditto	N/Nil
"	26.4.17		ditto	N/Nil
"	27.4.17		Inspection of horses by Lt Gen Cavanagh, G.O.C. Cav. Corps.	N/Nil
"	28.4.17		Routine & small works at LOUVENCOURT & VAUCHELLES	N/Nil
"	29.4.17		ditto	N/Nil
"	30.4.17		ditto	N/Nil

W Wathen-Jones
O.C. 4th Field Squadron R.E.

WAR DIARY

4TH
FIELD SQUADRON, R.E.,
4TH CAVALRY DIVISION.
W.D. 14/7
No.
Date April 1917

April 1917

Serial No. 148

4th Field Squadron, R.E.

From 1st May to 30th June 1917.

Daily list of
in Adjutant
----o

Issued to Section_____

From whom.	No. and date of letter received.

WAR DIARY or INTELLIGENCE SUMMARY

4th Field Coy
May 1917

Army Form C. 2118

Place	Date	Hour	Summary of Events and Information	Remarks and references to Appendices
MARIEUX	1.5.17		'B' Tp. rode to HEM to bridging practice. Billeting took at LOUVENCOURT	N.R.
"	2.5.17		Evening 2 Nissen huts to A.S.C.	N.R.
"	3.5.17		Stable return at VAUCHELLES	N.R.
"	4.5.17		ditto	N.R.
"	5.5.17		Sections carried out bridging practice at HEM. VAUCHELLES work continued	N.R.
"	6.5.17		Billeting took in MARIEUX. VAUCHELLES work continued.	N.R.
"	7.5.17		Electric lighting circuit MARIEUX started VAUCHELLES work continued. Emmanuel installing Chofs meter at BEAUQUESNE	N.R.
"	8.5.17		Same work as previous day. Carried out experiments with D.M. to simplify bridging equipment. Lt M Sinclair D.S.O. R.E. & Ct Edmond R.E. from G. H.Q. on present	N.R.
			Received orders to move into to more site at Army, and c repetition to work L.t C.R.E. Cav Corps. the 48 D.M.	N.R.
MEAULTE	9.5.17		Squadron marched to MEAULTE there it WHQ.	N.R.
BRIE	10.5.17		Squadron marched to BRIE 5 miles S of PERONNE where it camped. Main Pints Lieut R.E. & Lieut Bonnes went and Divisional area with a view to setting camps for the division there it moves up.	N.R.
BRIE	11.5.17		Lt Gordon & Lt Graham reconnoitre watering facilities in area. Major Rains & Kee R.E. met C.R.E. Can Corps. & started camp for Field Squadron at FOURQUES & settled positions of all troops to which existed when march up from senewal plan for D.H.Q. Camp at ATHIES. Men employed on collecting hut material etc	N.R.
FOURQUES	12.5.17		Squadron marched to FOURQUES Lt Graham & A Tp. commenced watering troughs in MESNIL area Lt Gordon & 6 C Tp. Ter down on ENNEMAIN - ST CHRIST area. Lt Lloyd & B Tp. commenced work on D.H.Q. Camp at ATHIES - other huts commenced by D.M. at MEAULTE.	N.R.

Army Form C. 2118

WAR DIARY
or
INTELLIGENCE SUMMARY
(Erase heading not required.)

Instructions regarding War Diaries and Intelligence Summaries are contained in F.S. Regs, Part II. and the Staff Manual respectively. Title Pages will be prepared in manuscript.

Place	Date	Hour	Summary of Events and Information	Remarks and references to Appendices
FOURQUES	13.5.17		Work continued as on 12th inst. Very heavy gale of wind causes considerable delay, his lot at Camp (D.H.Q.) owing to wet state of winter being available over the face of the country.	Rd. Nk.
"	14.5.17		Work continued on the 13th inst. Further delay in work at D.H.Q. camp owing to wet state of material, &c.	Rd. Nk.
"	15.5.17		Received orders to and 2 & 3 Dismounted troops to work in preparation with 5th Field Squadron. Work continued on 14th inst with addition to & Nissen huts for Bde. Hqs. Work commenced at ST CHRIST un MESNIL. Between 12 huts & enemy. 7.13.K. all D.H., and & working parts of S.O.R. & 17th Lanc. in Lt. Spearmen - their huts had been dismantled; huts at MESNIL & sending them up.	Rd. Nk.
"	16.5.17		2 Lt. Graham & A Tp, 2 Lt. Bennett & B Tp, 2 Lt. Gunton & C Tp, (amongst strength 20 Sapper ranks & tools wagons & damage to horses) proceeded to from St Givre Squadron at JEANCOURT, R 15 a.9.5, & MONTIGNY FM respectively. By the first evening arrangements were practically completed. 2nd. Lt. Capt. Brooke has since no worth with his group. Work in Camp D. Hqs MESNIL (for LUCKNOW Bde Hqs & 70 Tk run Sector - Lu (Pertab Singh), & ST CHRIST un Sector was continued with organized a necessary reduction of hutting in these corners, also further below in the preparation of the Camps.	M Nk.

Army Form C. 2118.

WAR DIARY
or
INTELLIGENCE SUMMARY.
(Erase heading not required.)

Instructions regarding War Diaries and Intelligence Summaries are contained in F. S. Regs., Part II, and the Staff Manual respectively. Title pages will be prepared in manuscript.

Hour, Date, Place.	Summary of Events and Information.	Remarks and references to Appendices.
FOURQUES 17.5.17.	Work in Camp at MESNIL & ENNEMAIN & at Divl Hqs camp at ATHIES.	N.M.
" 18.5.17.	2/Lt LLOYD & 7 O.R. proceeds to track area to dismantle Asian huts & send to Inf. Work as for previous day.	N.M.
" 19.5.17.	Work as before, with addition of 1 Nissen hut sent to 1st Amstrala. & Sialket Cavly Field Ambulance.	N.M.
" 20.5.17.	Work as before.	N.M.
" 21.5.17.	Major Raikes & Capt Buchanan went round 16th Bde Sectn with a view to taking over work when 4th Cav Div relieve that bright.	N.M.
" 22.5.17.	Work — sectn of 3 troops (100') between BRIE & ST CHRIST. 3 troops with 5th Cav Div regiments moving to: — C Tmp. TEMPLEUX B — ROISEL A — JEANCOURT.	N.M.
" 23.5.17.	5 O.R. proceeds to HERVILLY to work on Divl Hq camp there. Sgt Hope moved to ROISEL. Major Raikes accompanied S.O.E. (Majr En Kennedy) round intermediate — deciding what work was required in the I left of the section.	N.M.

Army Form C. 2118.

WAR DIARY
or
INTELLIGENCE SUMMARY.
(Erase heading not required.)

Instructions regarding War Diaries and Intelligence Summaries are contained in F. S. Regs., Part II, and the Staff Manual respectively. Title pages will be prepared in manuscript.

Hour, Date, Place.	Summary of Events and Information.	Remarks and references to Appendices.
ROISEL 24.5.17.	Two sections of 469th Field. Coy. attached to superior both of mining Personnel. lui — this work started tonight	WNK
" 25.5.17.	1200' of sunk upon farm completes opposite FERVAQUE FARM	WNK.
" 26.5.17.	both continued	WNK.
" 27.5.17.	Mining continued	WNK.
" 28.5.17.	ditto	WNK.
" 29.5.17.	ditto — 2 sections 469th Fld. (. Cof. rejoin this unit both on intermediate line.	WNK.
" 30.5.17.	ditto	WNK.
" 31.5.17.	ditto	WNK.

W Walker
Major R.E.
O.C. 4th Richard Brown R.E.
31/5/17

Army Form C. 2118

WAR DIARY
or
INTELLIGENCE SUMMARY
(Erase heading not required.)

Instructions regarding War Diaries and Intelligence Summaries are contained in F.S. Regs., Part II. and the Staff Manual respectively. Title Pages will be prepared in manuscript.

Place	Date	Hour	Summary of Events and Information	Remarks and references to Appendices
ROISEL	1.6.17		Work continued on intermediate line, dug-outs in Quarry.	Rank
"	2.6.17		ditto	R.S.K.
"	3.6.17		ditto	Rank
"	4.6.17		ditto	Rank
"	5.6.17		ditto	Rank
"	6.6.17		ditto	Rank
"	7.6.17		ditto	Rank
"	8.6.17		ditto	Rank
"	9.6.17		ditto	Rank
"	10.6.17		ditto	Rank
"	11.6.17		ditto	Rank
"	12.6.17		ditto	Rank
"	13.6.17		ditto	Rank
"	14.6.17		ditto	Rank
"	15.6.17		Capt Buchanan transferred to Headquarters 3rd Field Squadron R.E.	Rank
"	16.6.17		ditto	Rank
"	17.6.17		ditto	Rank
"	18.6.17		ditto	Rank
"	19.6.17		ditto	Rank
"	20.6.17		ditto	Rank
"	21.6.17		ditto	Rank
"	22.6.17		ditto	Rank

Army Form C. 2118

WAR DIARY
or
INTELLIGENCE SUMMARY

(Erase heading not required.)

Instructions regarding War Diaries and Intelligence Summaries are contained in F. S. Regs., Part II. and the Staff Manual respectively. Title Pages will be prepared in manuscript.

Place	Date	Hour	Summary of Events and Information	Remarks and references to Appendices
ROISEL	23.6.17		Work continues on transcript (main) Reports i training outpost line. 2/Lieut LLOYD furnish dump for transcript at HERVILLY with 2 platoons of B.	Men
"	24.6.17		ditto dump	ditto
"	25.6.17		ditto	ditto
"	26.6.17		ditto	ditto
"	27.6.17		ditto	ditto
"	28.6.17		ditto	ditto
"	29.6.17		ditto	ditto
"	30.6.17		ditto	ditto

U. Robertson
Major R.E.
O.C. 4th Field Coy R.E.

Serial No: **148.**

4th Field Squadron, R.E.

From 1st to 31st July 1917.

Daily list of
in Adjutant

Issued to Section_____

From whom.	No. and date of letter received.

Army Form C. 2118

SECRET

1st Field Sqdn. R.E.

WAR DIARY
or
INTELLIGENCE SUMMARY
(Erase heading not required.)

Instructions regarding War Diaries and Intelligence Summaries are contained in F.S. Regs., Part II. and the Staff Manual respectively. Title Pages will be prepared in manuscript.

Place	Date	Hour	Summary of Events and Information	Remarks and references to Appendices
ROISEL	1.7.17		Work continued on Hermadale line, & dugouts. 2/Lt LLOYD R.E. & 11 Sappers took part in raid on COLOGNE FARM in company with 2 platoons of the 6th INNISKILLING DRAGOONS. Bangalore torpedos though carried were not required, but 330 lb of Ammonal & Guncotton were successfully exploded in M.G. gun emplacements, dugouts and cellars. Time allowed for demolition was rather short as R.E. had only 22 minutes to complete their demolitions.	Ack.
"	2.7.17		Work continued on Hermadale line, & wiring & outpost line, & dugouts.	Ack.
"	3.7.17		ditto	Ack.
"	4.7.17		ditto	Ack.
"	5.7.17		ditto	Ack.
"	6.7.17		ditto	Ack.
"	7.7.17		ditto. Two dugouts Lacartoiné & mining shaft put in with 2 months charge. Two dugouts on the right. Objection on extreme M.G. emplacement near from B. on bank. FALLEN TREES. Owing to heavy hostile fire trenches were not reached.	Ack.

WAR DIARY
or
INTELLIGENCE SUMMARY

(Erase heading not required.)

Army Form C. 2118

Place	Date	Hour	Summary of Events and Information	Remarks and references to Appendices
ROISEL	8.7.17.		Work on Intermediate line, strong pts continued.	Nil.
FOURQUES	9.7.17.		Squadron (less 2 men on Attachment with Farms Officer) on courses as regards duties.	Nil.
"	10.7.17.		Work on D.H.Q. camp ATHIES – checking equipment etc.	Nil.
"	11.7.17.		Squadron Drill. Billetting work & roads.	Nil.
"	12.7.17.		" " " " & roads.	Nil.
"	13.7.17.		" " " " " Lt GRAHAM R.E.	Nil.
"	14.7.17.		proceeds on detachment to 1st Cavalry Corps.	Nil.
"	15.7.17.		Billetting work, preparation for D.I. Horse show	Nil.
"	16.7.17.		ditto	Nil.
"	17.7.17.		ditto	Nil.
"	18.7.17.		ditto	Nil.
"	19.7.17.		ditto	Nil.

Army Form C. 2118

WAR DIARY
or
INTELLIGENCE SUMMARY
(Erase heading not required.)

Instructions regarding War Diaries and Intelligence Summaries are contained in F. S. Regs., Part II. and the Staff Manual respectively. Title Pages will be prepared in manuscript.

Place	Date	Hour	Summary of Events and Information	Remarks and references to Appendices
FOURQUES	20.	7.17	Battalion hutting work, preparation for O.V.I. some shown	much
"	21.	7.17	d/to	much
"	22.	7.17	d/to	much
"	23.	7.17	d/to	much
"	24.	7.17	d/to	much
"	25.	7.17	} Divisional horse show	much
"	26.	7.17	Battalion - hutting work	much
"	27.	7.17	d/to	much
"	28.	7.17	d/to	much
"	29.	7.17	d/to. preparation of book, and rabies prints.	much
"	30.	7.	d/to	"
"	31.	7.2	d/to	much

O.C. 4th [signature]

1875 W. W593/826 1,000,000 4/15 J.B.C. & A. A.D.S.S./Forms/C. 2118.

Serial No: **148.**

4th Field Squadron, R.E.

From 1st to 31st August 1917.

Army Form C. 2118

WAR DIARY
or
INTELLIGENCE SUMMARY
(Erase heading not required.)

Instructions regarding War Diaries and Intelligence Summaries are contained in F. S. Regs., Part II. and the Staff Manual respectively. Title Pages will be prepared in manuscript.

Place	Date	Hour	Summary of Events and Information	Remarks and references to Appendices
FOURQUES	1.8.17		Hutting & billetting work - Squadron mounted sports - rest day.	nok.
"	2.8.17		ditto. Commenced training programmes for October.	nok.
"	3.8.17		ditto. Squadron Drill.	nok.
"	4.8.17		ditto. Commenced battle brigade at ENNEMAIN. Squadron Drill.	nok.
"	5.8.17		ditto. Squadron Drill.	nok.
"	6.8.17		Squadron Drill, driving Drill. Hutting work as before	nok.
"	7.8.17		Hutting work. R.Dvy. school. Bridge at ENNEMAIN finished.	nok.
"	8.8.17		Lt. Gaston with C Tp. & 2.Lt Edmond with B Tp. proceeded on Ithakhorn to 33rd Div. Hutting work.	nok.
"	9.8.17		Hutting & ENNEMAIN ratrines. To CHRIST & MONS. Billetting work.	nok. nok.
"	10.8.17		as before	nok. nok.
"	11.8.17		as before	nok. nok.
"	12.8.17		as before	nok. nok.
"	13.8.17		as before	nok.
"	14.8.17		as before - preparing material for bridge over OMIGNON BRIG	nok.
"	15.8.17		as before	ST CHRIST nok.
"	16.8.17		as before	nok.
"	17.8.17		as before	nok.

1873 W: W593/826 1,000,000 4/15 J.B.C. & A. A.D.S.S./Forms/C. £118.

Army Form C. 2118

WAR DIARY
or
INTELLIGENCE SUMMARY
(Erase heading not required.)

Instructions regarding War Diaries and Intelligence Summaries are contained in F. S. Regs., Part II. and the Staff Manual respectively. Title Pages will be prepared in manuscript.

Place	Date	Hour	Summary of Events and Information	Remarks and references to Appendices
FOURQUES	18.8.17		Halting & Wiltating work. Bridge on OM19/1031 started at 10.30 am G	M.W.
"	19.8.17		Rear of 4th Army traffic by 8 p.m.	M.W.
"	20.8.17		Bridge finished & other work on hopes.	M.W.
"	21.8.17		ditto	M.W.
"	22.8.17		ditto – 2 troops returns from 3rd Division	M.W.
			Lt S.G. Bennett & party from A Troop proceeds with 4th Division Bridge to 34th Div. area.	
"	23.8.17		#Lt J.H. Garden, relieves Lt Bennett. Ration.	M.W.
"	24.8.17			M.W.
"	25.8.17		Lt S.G. Bennett with 42 O.R. & 45 horses left for S.A.B. with a view to completing m' Cav. Cops. there then.	M.W.
"	26.8.17		Halting work.	M.W.
"	27.8.17		ditto.	M.W.
"	28.8.17		Halting & Wiltating work.	M.W.
"	29.8.17		ditto	M.W.
"	30.8.17		ditto	M.W.
"	31.8.17		ditto	M.W.

Rec'd 1.9.17 HQ

W. Mitchener Major
O.C. 4th Field Sqn. M.

Army Form C. 2118.

1917 4th Field Squadron R.E.
Serial No. 148

WAR DIARY
or
INTELLIGENCE SUMMARY.
(Erase heading not required.)

Instructions regarding War Diaries and Intelligence Summaries are contained in F. S. Regs., Part II. and the Staff Manual respectively. Title pages will be prepared in manuscript.

Place	Date	Hour	Summary of Events and Information	Remarks and references to Appendices
FOURQUES.	Sept. 1.		B Troop motor 2/Lt S.C. BENNETT, R.E. inc. Field Troop. Event m/c Cmdrs into strenua line.	over
"	2		General work in camp.	over
"	3		General work in camp.	over
"	4		ditto	over
"	5		ditto	over
"	6		ditto	over
"	7		ditto	over
"	8		ditto	over
"	9		Laying out of intbln Camps commenced. General work in camps. 2/Lt Renault started	over
"	10		Reconnaissance by S.C. Cav. Div. training area.	over
"	11		Work proceeded with in above.	over
"	12		ditto	over
"	13		ditto	over
"	14		ditto	over
"	15		ditto	over work

WAR DIARY or INTELLIGENCE SUMMARY

Army Form C. 2118.

(Erase heading not required.)

Place	Date	Hour	Summary of Events and Information	Remarks and references to Appendices
FAUQUES	Sept 16		Laying out of winter Camps continued.	2.P/4
	17		C.R.E. Cavalry Corps Lt. Col. W H EVANS joined the Squadron to take charge of camping work.	2.P/4
	18		Detachments of 2nd, 3rd, 4 & 5th Field Squadrons arrive to do winter hutting in 5 Cav. Division	2.P/4
	19		2/Lt. A.R.S. EDWARDS 4 2nd C.R. go to MONTECOURT on detachment to do winter hutting for 5 Cav. Div.	2.P/4
	20		Work on winter huttings continued.	2.P/4
	21		ditto	2.P/4
	22		ditto	2.P/4
	23		ditto	2.P/4
	24		ditto	2.P/4
	25		2/Lt. J.A. GRAHAM promoted full Lieut. dating from 1-7-17.	2.P/4
	26		Capt. (temp. Major) R.S. RATTRKERR left the Squadron to proceed to INDIA.	2.P/4
	27		Work on hutting continued	2.P/4
	28		ditto	2.P/4
	29		2/Lt. S.G. BENNETT promoted full Lieut. dating from 1-7-17.	2.P/4
	30		Work on hutting continued	2.P/4

Army Form C. 2118.

148

4th Field Squadron

WAR DIARY
or
INTELLIGENCE SUMMARY.
(Erase heading not required.)

1917

Place	Date	Hour	Summary of Events and Information	Remarks and references to Appendices
FOUQUES	Oct/Nov 1		Major A.J.S. HILL RE took over command of 4th Field Squadron.	
"	2		Winter hutting continued.	
"	3			
"	4		C.R.E. Car conveying Lt. Col. H. EVANS returned at Car Dep. H.Q.	
"	5		Work on bridges, trenches & entrenchment.	ditto
"	6			ditto
"	7			ditto
"	8		1 British Officer & 35 O.R. Native Cavalry attached to 4 FS for billet	
"	9		for Border Mounted Infantry on leave.	ditto
"	10			ditto
"	11			ditto
"	12			ditto
"	13			ditto
"	14			ditto
"	15			ditto
"	16			ditto

Army Form C. 2118.

WAR DIARY
or
INTELLIGENCE SUMMARY.

(Erase heading not required.)

Instructions regarding War Diaries and Intelligence Summaries are contained in F. S. Regs., Part II and the Staff Manual respectively. Title pages will be prepared in manuscript.

Place	Date	Hour	Summary of Events and Information	Remarks and references to Appendices
FOURAVEL	Dx 17		Work on winter hutting continued	S.H.W
"	18		ditto	S.H.W
"	19		ditto	S.H.W
"	20		ditto	S.H.W
"	21		ditto	S.H.W
"	22		ditto	S.H.W
"	23		ditto	S.H.W
"	24		ditto	S.H.W
"	25		To PERONNE PLATEAU and FROISSY transport to FORT	S.H.W
"	26		ditto & Curl huttes entries	B.H.W
"	27		Major Smith proceeded to ENGLAND. Lift huttLERs commencing Day	B.H.W
"	28		Work on Winter hutting continued	B.H.W
"	29		ditto	B.H.W
"	30		Work on Divisional School at SAVEURS started	B.H.W
"	31		Work on Winter hutting continued	B.H.W

J.W.Walsh
C.R.E.
4TH CAVALRY DIVISION.

Army Form C. 2118.

WAR DIARY
or
INTELLIGENCE SUMMARY.

(Erase heading not required.)

148

4th FA Ajan
1917

Place	Date	Hour	Summary of Events and Information	Remarks and references to Appendices
Tangier	Nov 1st		Winter hutting continued	R 143
"	2		ditto	
"	3		ditto	
"	4		ditto	
"	5		ditto	
"	6		ditto	
"	7		Major H.F.S. Hill came back from leave & resumed command	R110
"	8		Winter hutting continued	a73H
"	9		ditto	a73H
"	10		ditto	a73H
"	11		ditto	a73H
"	12		ditto	a73H
"	13		do	a73H
"	14		do	a73H
"	15		do	a73H
"	16		do	a73H

Army Form C. 2118.

WAR DIARY
or
INTELLIGENCE SUMMARY.
(Erase heading not required.)

Place	Date	Hour	Summary of Events and Information	Remarks and references to Appendices
FOURQUES	17/11/17		Work on hut building continued.	APP 14
"	18		ditto	APP 14
"	19		Work on hut building also continued and marching drill continued. Camp fatigues and various fatigues. "B" troop with Lt Crawford joined LUCKNOW BRIGADE	APP 14
"	20		Squadron was placed under 2 hour notice to proceed in direction of CAMBRAI.	APP 14
"	21		Squadron marched to FINS. (Battle of CAMBRAI).	APP 14 & APP 14
FINS	22		"B" Troop rejoined Squadron at FINS camp.	APP 14
FINS	23		Squadron returned to FOURQUES camp	APP 14
FOURQUES	24		Squadron ordered with 4th Cav. Div. to VILLERS FOUCON attack	APP 14
"	25		Work on hut building recommenced.	APP 14
"	26		do do do continued.	APP 14
"	27		do do do	APP 14
"	28		do do do	APP 14
"	29		Squadron marched to VILLERS-FOUCON with Division. B troop detached to MHOW Brigade.	APP 14

Army Form C. 2118.

WAR DIARY
or
INTELLIGENCE SUMMARY.
(Erase heading not required.)

Instructions regarding War Diaries and Intelligence Summaries are contained in F. S. Regs., Part II. and the Staff Manual respectively. Title pages will be prepared in manuscript.

Place	Date	Hour	Summary of Events and Information	Remarks and references to Appendices
VILLERS FAUCON	Nov 3rd		B Troop changed WR FROM Bryfield. No casualties.	APPX

A J Hill
Major RE
OC 4th Field Squadron

Army Form C. 2118.

4TH
"Army Form C. 2118.
4TH CAVALRY DIVISION

WAR DIARY
or
INTELLIGENCE SUMMARY.

(Erase heading not required.)

Instructions regarding War Diaries and Intelligence Summaries are contained in F. S. Regs., Part II. and the Staff Manual respectively. Title pages will be prepared in manuscript.

4 Field Squadron R.E.
4 Cav Div

Place	Date	Hour	Summary of Events and Information	Remarks and references to Appendices
VILLERS FAUCON	Dec 1st		Sq. 2 works on a string point near at VAUCELETTE FARM at night	62A
"	2nd		do	62A
"	3rd		do	62A
HEUDICOURT	4th		Squadron moved to HEUDICOURT, one N.F.A. manoeuvre	62A
"	5th		do	62A
"	6th		do	62A
FOURQUES	7th		Squadron returned to ATHIES (FOURQUES) (winter training continues)	62A
"	8th		do	62A
"	9th		do	62A
"	10th		do	62A
"	11th		do	62A
"	12th		do	62A
"	13th		do	62A
"	14th		do	62A

Army Form C. 2118.

WAR DIARY
or
INTELLIGENCE SUMMARY.
(Erase heading not required.)

Instructions regarding War Diaries and Intelligence Summaries are contained in F. S. Regs., Part II. and the Staff Manual respectively. Title pages will be prepared in manuscript.

Place	Date	Hour	Summary of Events and Information	Remarks and references to Appendices
ROISEL	15th Dec		Work on trench hutting continued	A.P.J.A.
"	16th		do	A.P.J.A.
"	17th		do. 13 Re enforcements from 2nd P.S.	A.P.J.A.
"	18th		Work on trench hutting continued	A.P.J.A.
"	19th		do	A.P.J.A.
"	20th		do	A.P.J.A.
"	21st		do	A.P.J.A.
"	22nd		do	A.P.J.A.
"	23rd		do	A.P.J.A.
"	24th		do	A.P.J.A.
"	25th		do.	Q.H.W.
"	26th		do.	Q.H.W.
"	27th		do.	Q.H.W.
"	28th		do.	Q.H.W.
"	29th		Major A.F.S. HILL went to BOUVINCOURT as C.R.E. Dismounted Division	Q.H.W.
"	30th		Lt. K.M. MACDOWELL went with "C" Troop to HERVILLY to work on the line	Q.H.W.
"	31st		2Lt. LLOYD joined. Major HILL at Ad Ao. QUIVINCOURT (?)	Q.H.W.

O.O. 4TH FIELD SQUADRON R.E.
4TH CAVALRY DIVISION

Army Form C. 2118.

WAR DIARY
or
INTELLIGENCE SUMMARY. 4th Field Squadron RE
(Erase heading not required.) 4 Jan 1916

Instructions regarding War Diaries and Intelligence Summaries are contained in F.S. Regs., Part II. and the Staff Manual respectively. Title pages will be prepared in manuscript.

Place	Date	Hour	Summary of Events and Information	Remarks and references to Appendices
FOURQUES	Jan 1st		January 1916 Work on winter hutting continued	Diary (1)
"	2nd		"	Diary (2)
"	3rd		"	Diary (3)
"	4th		"	Diary (4)
"	5th		2Lt. DISNEY rejoined from detachment	Diary (5)
"	6th		2Lt. EDWARDS joined. Lt. McDOWELL at JEANCOURT hutting continued	Diary (6)
"	7th		"	Diary (7)
"	8th		"	Diary (8)
"	9th		"	Diary (9)
"	10th		"	Diary (10)
"	11th		"	Diary (11)
"	12th		Lt. McDOWELL joined. Major MILNE at BOUVINCOURT work on winter hutting continued	Diary (12)
"	13th		"	Diary (13)
"	14th		"	Diary (14)
"	15th		"	Diary (15)

Army Form C. 2118.

WAR DIARY
or
INTELLIGENCE SUMMARY.   4th Field Squadron. A.E.

(Erase heading not required.)

Instructions regarding War Diaries and Intelligence Summaries are contained in F. S. Regs., Part II and the Staff Manual respectively. Title pages will be prepared in manuscript.

Place	Date	Hour	Summary of Events and Information	Remarks and references to Appendices
FourDues	Jan 16		Work on winter hutting continued	App III
"	17		"	App III
"	18		"	App III
"	19		"	App III
"	20		"	App III
"	21		"	App III
"	22		"	App III
"	23		"	App III
"	24		"	App III
"	25		"	App III
"	26		"	App III
"	27		"	App III
"	28		Mr. J. A. GRAHAM joined. Major HILL at BOUZINCOURT, CAPT. H.J. KEANE R.A.M.C. left the Squadron to join Lucknow C.F.A.	App III

Army Form C. 2118.

WAR DIARY
or
~~INTELLIGENCE SUMMARY~~ 4th Field Squadron RE

(Erase heading not required.)

Instructions regarding War Diaries and Intelligence
Summaries are contained in F. S. Regs., Part II.
and the Staff Manual respectively. Title pages
will be prepared in manuscript.

Place	Date	Hour	Summary of Events and Information	Remarks and references to Appendices
FOURQUES	Jan 29th		Work on winter hutting continued	P.4.W
"	30th		"	P.4.W
"	31st		"	P.4.W

R H Wallow
Capt. R.E.
OC 4 Field Squadron

Army Form C. 2118.

WAR DIARY or INTELLIGENCE SUMMARY.

Hd. Field Squadron R.E.
1st Can. Div.
February 1918.
B.E.F. 865

Place	Date	Hour	Summary of Events and Information	Remarks and references to Appendices
FOURDRINOY	Feb 1st		Hutting work discontinued owing to move of 4th Cav Div. Work carried out in camp ends; Hut Mess/Hut M.O./ Hut 75/45 Engineers	
"	2nd		Lt. J.A. GRAHAM moved to VADENCOURT	
"	3rd		Lt. J.A. GRAHAM moved to VADENCOURT 1st & 7th Old M.G.Y. work in camp continued	
"	4th		"	
"	5th		Attached to 2 Field Sqdn work have been built the alien	
"	6th		Hutting work recommenced for 2nd Cav Div	
"	7th		Hutting work continued	
"	8th		"	
"	9th		"	
"	10th		Lt. J.A. GRAHAM rejoined Squadron at FOURDRINOY	
"	11th		Lt. J.A. GRAHAM proceeded on leave to U.K.	
"	12th		Hutting work continued	
"	13th		"	
DEVISE	14th		The Squadron less lines moved to new camp East of DEVISE. "B" Troop found C Troop at VADENCOURT with II in ORESNEY. Lt. EDWARDS rejoined Squadron at DEVISE.	

O.W.D. Edwards
Major R.E.
O.C. 4th FIELD SQUADRON R.E.
4TH CAVALRY DIVISION.

Army Form C. 2118.

WAR DIARY
or
INTELLIGENCE=SUMMARY.
(Erase heading not required.)

4 Field Squadron

Place	Date	Hour	Summary of Events and Information	Remarks and references to Appendices
DENIZE	Feb 15th		Work in camp carried out	
"	16th		"	
"	17th		"	
"	18th		"	
"	19th		"	
"	20th		"	
"	21st		"	
"	22nd		The Squadron packed up preparatory to moving	
BRUSLE	23rd		The Squadron moved to new billets in BRUSLE	
"	24th		Capt. F.J.H. WALLER proceeded on leave to U.K. Lt A.B.D. EDWARDS took over command of the Squadron in the back area	
	25th 26th		50 Riding horses transferred to O.D.R. Cavalry Corps. Work in camp carried out	
			CAPT. F.J.H. WALLER transferred to 5th FIELD SQUADRON.	
	27th		Work in camp carried out	
	28th		" " " "	
			Lt Ordrey transferred to MAISSE M.K.	

A.B.D. Edwards
O.C. 4TH FIELD SQUADRON R.E.
4TH CAVALRY DIVISION.

Army Form C. 2118.

148

WAR DIARY
INTELLIGENCE SUMMARY

1st Field Squadron R.E.
March 1916

(Erase heading not required.)

Place	Date	Hour	Summary of Events and Information	Remarks and references to Appendices
BRIE	1st		Capt. J.C. O'Connor joined Squadron as M.O. from 5th Field Sqn.	ADT
"	2nd		Lieut J.A. Graham returned from leave. 9 O.R's joined to Oudney at MAISSEMY	ADT
"	3rd		Lieut J.A. Graham proceeded to MAISSEMY to relieve Lt Oudney. W.O.R in camp.	ADT
"	4th		Lieut Oudney returned to Squadron. Interpreter Furlonnet to E. Batty RHA, 2nd Cav. Div.	Night
"	5th		Lt Oudney proceeded on leave to U.K. Work in camp.	ADT
"	6th		Squadron supplied with Hotchkiss Rifles. Work in camp	ADT
"	7th		Lt Graham returned with detachments from MAISSEMY and VADENCOURT	ADT
"	8th		Work in camp	ADT
"	9th		Major A.J.S. Ker, Lieut Medlycott and 2nd Lieut Lloyd reported Squadron with detachment from BOUVINCOURT.	ADT
"	10th		Work in camp	
"	11th		Work in camp. Capt. J.L. Forsyth joined Squadron from 2 Fd Sqn. Lieut H.A. Lloyd left Sqn & proceeded to Field Sqn. Work in camp.	ADT
"	12th		Lieut Babington joined Sqn from 1st Divl Sqn. Work in camp.	ADT
"	13th		Major A.S. Hill transferred to Cav. Corps. Squadron marched to BRIE.	p.5

MARCH 1918.

WAR DIARY of 4th Fd. Sqn. R.E.
INTELLIGENCE SUMMARY.

Army Form C. 2118.

(Erase heading not required.)

Place	Date	Hour	Summary of Events and Information	Remarks and references to Appendices
BRIE	14th		The Squadron marched to BLAMGY-TRONVILLE	
BLAMGY-TRONVILLE	15		The Squadron marched to FERRIERES.	
FERRIERES	16		Squadron marched to BETTENCOURT	
BETTENCOURT	17		Work in Camp.	
"	18		Work in Camp. 9 Horses evacuated. Handed in Squadron Equipment	
"	19		Work in Camp. 9 wagons handed over at AMT. ABBEVILLE. about 14 horses	
"	20		Work in Camp. Part of Equipment handed over to D.A.D.O.S at Eu Dep	
"	21		Work in Camp. Lt Ouseley returned from leave. 14 horses transferred to Longpre Pk	
"	22		Work in Camp.	
"	23		Lt Bebington evacuated 19 horses to MARSEILLES. Lt Ouseley conducted 28 horses to DIEPPE	
"	24		Capt Montyll attended conference of Longpre Group Res at 2 DEPWSRATL.	
"			41 L.D. Horses proceeded to ABBEVILLE (No 2 Advance Remount Depot	
"	25		" Lt Ouseley & party returned from DIEPPE.	
"	26		Squadron marched to FAMECHON	
FAMECHON	27		Squadron marched to AILLY LE HAUT CLOCHER. Capt JPC Connor R.H.T.C left.	

Army Form C. 2118.

"WAR DIARY of 4th Field Squadron R.E.
INTELLIGENCE SUMMARY.

(Erase heading not required.)

Instructions regarding War Diaries and Intelligence Summaries are contained in F.S. Regs., Part II. and the Staff Manual respectively. Title pages will be prepared in manuscript.

March 1918.

Place	Date	Hour	Summary of Events and Information	Remarks and references to Appendices
AILLY LE HAUT CLOCHER	28th		Work in Camp. Musketry Training	M
"	29		Work in Camp. Musketry Training	
"	30		Graham to Demobilisation	
"	31		Musketry Training; Work in Camp.	

[signature]
Capt. R.E.
MAJOR, R.E.
O.C. 4TH FIELD SQUADRON,
4TH CAVALRY DIVISION.

31/3/18

Army Form C. 2118.

WAR DIARY 1st Field Squadron R.E.
or
INTELLIGENCE SUMMARY.
(Erase heading not required.)

April 1918

Place	Date	Hour	Summary of Events and Information	Remarks and references to Appendices
Ailly le Haut Clocher	1st		Musketry & Physical Training	
"	2nd		Musketry & Physical Training	
"	3rd		Musketry & Physical Training, Demolitions etc	
"	4th		Musketry & Field Works	
"			Musketry & Field Works	
			Lieut McDowell Transferred to 2nd Field Squadron R.E.	
			Lieut Babington rejoined Squadron from Marseilles	
"	5th		Musketry & Field Works	
			Field Works Demolitions & Musketry Training	
	6th		Physical Drill & Field Works	
	7th		Physical Drill & Musketry Training	
	8th		Physical Drill & Musketry Training	
	9th		Physical Drill & Musketry Training	
	10th		Physical Drill Route March	
	11th		Coy formed with 1st Lgt Squadron, 67th R.H.A. H.Q. 231 Cy Regt	
	12th		Physical Drill & Musketry	
	13th		Physical Drill & Musketry	
			Physical Drill Musketry & Route March	

2353 Wt. W2544/1454 700,000 5/15 D. D. & L. A.D.S.S. Forms/C. 2118.

WAR DIARY
or
INTELLIGENCE SUMMARY.

(Erase heading not required.)

4th Field Squadron R.E. Army Form C. 2118.

April 1918

Place	Date	Hour	Summary of Events and Information	Remarks and references to Appendices
Ailly le Haute Clocher	14th		Musketry. Route March.	
"	15th	10.45	Squadron left AILLEY LE HAUTE CLOCHIER for ABBEVILLE on Route for FARR	
			Squadron entrained at ABBEVILLE at 5 p.m. Train left for Rouen at 9 p.m.	
	16th		Squadron detrained at Rouen at 4 p.m. and marched to R.E. Base depot arriving at the camp at about 8 p.m.	
	17th		9a Camp Renewing Kit etc.	
	18th		9a Camp	
	19th		9a Camp	
	20th		Lt BABINGTON 9261 OUDNEY and all O.R. 67 4th Field Squadron transferred to R.E. Base Depot. Squadron ceased to exist.	

O.C. 4th Field Squadron R.E.

www.ingramcontent.com/pod-product-compliance
Lightning Source LLC
Chambersburg PA
CBHW081244170426
43191CB00034B/2034